Curious George®
Plants a Seed

Adaptation by Erica Zappy
Based on the TV series teleplay
written by Sandra Willard

Houghton Mifflin Company
Boston 2007

D0049741

For information about permission to reproduce selections from this book, write to Permissions, Houghton Mifflin Company, 215 Park Avenue South, New York, New York 10003.

Library of Congress Cataloging-in-Publication data
Zappy, Erica.
Curious George plants a seed / adaptation by Erica Zappy ; based on the TV series teleplay written by Sandra Willard.
p. cm.
ISBN-13: 978-0-618-77710-5 (pbk. : alk. paper)
ISBN-10: 0-618-77710-5 (pbk. : alk. paper)
I. Willard, Sandra. II. Curious George (Television program) III. Title.
PZ7.Z2583Cup 2007
[Fic]—dc22
2006036470

Design by Joyce White

www.houghtonmifflinbooks.com

Manufactured in China
WKT 10 9 8 7 6 5 4 3 2 1

Jumpy Squirrel was very busy.
George was curious.
What was Jumpy doing?

Bill, the boy next door, told George,
"Jumpy buries acorns and nuts.
He stores them in the ground.

He can dig them up later, when he is hungry."

That gave George
a great idea!
George buried the orange juice.

He buried the butter.
He buried the bread.
He was glad to find a
good place to store food.

When the man with the yellow hat came home, the kitchen was empty!

Where was all of their food?

George proudly showed his friend.

"George, orange juice and bread are not for burying," the man with the yellow hat said. "They cannot be stored in the ground."

His friend showed George
a peanut with a sprout.
George was puzzled.

"This peanut grew into a plant," the man said. "Seeds and nuts grow out of the ground, if they are not eaten first."

George thought he understood.
If a little peanut could become a big
plant, what would a rubber band
become?

What would a feather become?

George dug lots
of holes.
He buried lots
of things.

Soon the house was empty.
The man with the yellow hat was
surprised!

"George, umbrellas and chairs are
not for burying," the man with the
yellow hat explained.

"They are made by people. They are not going to grow. Seeds and nuts will grow."

A few days later George saw
something new in the yard.
It was a sprout!
"Look, George," said his friend.
"A seed you buried is growing!
I wonder what it will be."

Soon there was a beautiful
sunflower in the yard.
George had a green
thumb after all!

YOU CAN DO IT

GEORGE DISCOVERS THAT NOT EVERYTHING GROWS . . .
BUT SOME THINGS CERTAINLY DO!

If you'd like to grow something, try planting beans. In a few days, you'll have bean sprouts! You may need to ask a grownup for help with this exercise.

1. Fill a jar or plastic cup with half a cup of dried beans (a grownup can find these at the grocery store).

2. Cover them halfway with cool water.

3. Place a piece of nylon or cheesecloth on top of the cup and secure it with a rubber band.

4. Put it in a shady place for eight hours.

5. Gently drain the water through the cloth covering. Then add more water and immediately drain again.

6. Return the jar to the shady spot you found, but this time rest it on its side to give the beans more room to grow.

7. Rinse the beans twice a day for the next three days (as in step 5). After that, the sprouts will be ready to eat in a sandwich or salad! AND YOU GREW THEM YOURSELF!

WATER TRAIL

If you'd like to know how water helps a plant grow strong, find a piece of celery and some food coloring — then you can see for yourself!

1. Ask a grownup to cut a single stalk of celery for you that still has the leaves attached to the top.

2. Pick a food coloring (red or blue works best) and add some drops of it to a full glass of water.

3. Put the celery, leaves at the top, in the glass of water and leave it in a sunny place.

4. In a few hours, you might notice something different about the celery. Wait overnight.

5. The next day, check out your celery. It will be colorful! Ask a grownup to cut the celery in half for you. You'll see colored dots inside the celery. This is how you know water travels from the bottom of the stalk up to the leaf — the same way it travels up the stem of a flower—to help the celery grow strong!

Show what color your celery stalk became.

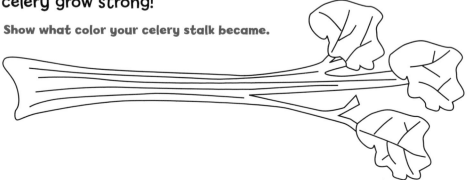